# Reconnecting with People

*A Strategy for Organization Success*

# Reconnecting with People

## *A Strategy for Organization Success*

Nancy Burzon
Jean Moore

Viva Books Private Limited
New Delhi • Mumbai • Chennai • Kolkata • Bangalore

First Indian Edition 2004

**VIVA BOOKS PRIVATE LIMITED**

- 4262/3 Ansari Road, Daryaganj, New Delhi 110 002
  E-mail: viva@vivagroupindia.net
- 215-216 New Apollo Estate, 2nd Floor, Mogra Lane, Andheri (E), Mumbai 400 069 E-mail: vivamumbai@vivagroupindia.net
- 7 Aziz Mulk, Seventh Street, Thousand Lights, Chennai 600 006
  E-mail: vivachennai@vivagroupindia.net
- B–103, Jindal Towers, 21/1A/3, Darga Road, Kolkata 700 017
  E-mail: vivakolkata@vivagroupindia.net
- 7 Sovereign Park Apts., 56-58 K. R. Road, Basavanagudi, Bangalore 560 004 Email: vivabangalore@vivagroupindia.net

*Published by arrangement with*

Crisp Publications. Inc.
1200 Hamilton Court,
Menlo Park
CA 94025
USA



ISBN 81-7649-653-7

Published by Vinod Vasishtha for Viva Books Private Limited, 4262/3 Ansari Road, Daryaganj, New Delhi 110 002 and printed at Raj Press, R-3 Inderpuri, New Delhi – 110012.

# CONTENTS

# Introduction

This book is written for people who want to achieve significant change, or transformation, in their organizations. It is based on the principle that people are more important than ever before to the success of the organization. In other words, the involvement of everyone in an organization is necessary during and after a change in order to achieve the desired objectives.

This book is not for people who believe that transformation can be achieved through acquisitions, divestitures or financial restructuring of the balance sheet. From our perspective, those strategies may be vital to an overall plan, but they are not sufficient by themselves.

From the mid-1980s to the mid-1990s, almost all North American corporations attempted some form of transformation in order to regain a competitive advantage. Other parts of the world were able to import manufactured goods into the United States at a lower price. These goods often were of higher quality than comparable U.S.-manufactured products. This presented an external challenge that many Americans had not faced before, and they looked to borrow some of the methods that had enabled the success of the new market entrants.

Significant focus was placed on *quality improvement* and related approaches of *process management* and *reengineering*. These efforts were oriented primarily around two objectives: 1) to eliminate defects from the products and the service delivery, and 2) to reduce costs by streamlining processes and eliminating all work that was not adding value to the product or service. These objectives are closely and positively related.

A result of these efforts was also an extensive downsizing of organizations. Remaining employees had to adjust to changing work structures, geographic relocation, combined organizations and new reporting relationships and team members. This upheaval, with its simultaneous environment of uncertainty, led to a reduction in employee loyalty. However, it also created an acceptance of ongoing change for the future in many organizations, particularly among management employees.

Hourly and union employees have not been as easily convinced of the need for transformation and its implications for them. They see the increased productivity and earnings growth experienced by many corporations as benefiting the shareholders and the senior management team at the expense of their job security and pension benefits.

Beginning in 1994, corporate strategy was influenced by Gary Hamel and C.K. Prahalad's book, *Competing for the Future*. They argued that companies cannot attain growth and long-term sustainability by a continuous focus on restructuring and reengineering. Instead, companies need to find ways to renew or regenerate themselves to avoid obsolescence. Hamel and Prahalad influenced our approach to providing support for the cultural transformation to be discussed in later chapters. Figure 1 illustrates this approach.

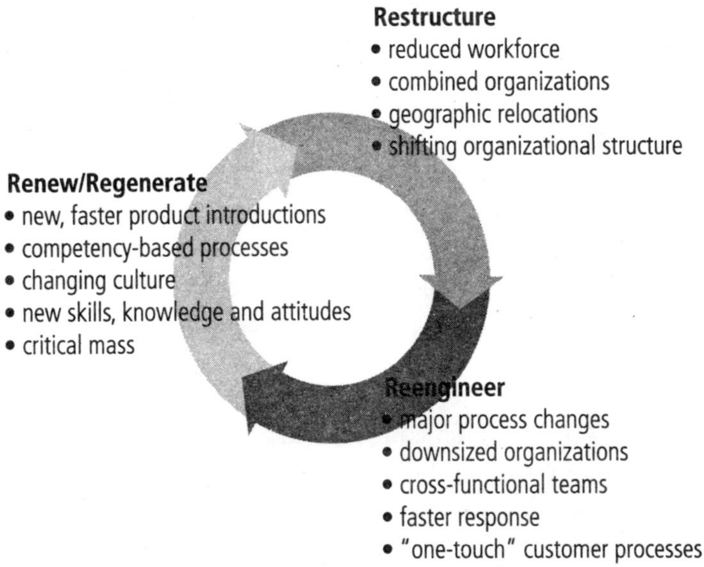


***Figure 1. Continuum of change for competitiveness***

As organizations work to implement this approach, they find the need for new knowledge, skills and attitudes takes a greater priority. In some industries, the competition for critical knowledge and skills is intense. The focus on renewal has also led to acquisitions as a means to grow revenues and earnings per share. This strategy is perceived more positively by employees when it is accompanied by restructuring, reorganizing and, ultimately, downsizing of the non-value-added parts of the business.

This continuous restructuring and reengineering brings to the organization benefits of efficiency, revenue growth and cost reduction. However, internal data indicate that employee attitudes and perceptions suffer in response to work load increases, constant change without involvement, and an environment of uncertainty and insecurity that accompanies these initiatives. Although management frequently says that employees are the most important asset in their business, management's actions, such as downsizing and restructuring, suggest that employees are expendable. Consequently, growing cynicism is apparent in many organizations. This is unhealthy for the work environment, but the implications go beyond the workplace.

There is a close, positive correlation between employee opinion of a company and customer perceptions. If employees feel that they are not providing quality products and services, customers will share that opinion. With that correlation, it becomes imperative to have employees "with you" during the transformation. They need to remain positive about the changes, seeing them as necessary for the good of the firm and its stakeholders. Internal employee surveys become an important indicator of both employee and customer perceptions.

By and large, any sustainable change strategy will be linked to growth. High-performing companies grow. Companies cannot downsize their way to profitability over time. Because growth strategies are more motivating to employees than is the death-spiral of continuous downsizing, it is no wonder that growth companies attract and retain the best employees.

Growth companies do many things to sustain high performance. A major factor is the articulation of a clear vision and direction for the company, widely shared and communicated within the organization. But the true differentiator, so often ignored, includes a human resources (HR) strategy aligned to that vision. Truly innovative companies today have revamped their HR departments to minimize the traditional administrative role and maximize the consultative role. They place far more emphasis on change management and organization development competencies for their HR professionals.

The creative HR organizations today have become invaluable business partners, with clear strategies to attract, train, motivate, promote and retain the best and the brightest in their respective industries. In today's competitive environment, companies without a clearly aligned HR strategy find themselves left struggling to compete for needed talent. Chapter 2 provides a detailed look at the HR role in an overall workforce blueprint for success.

The need for transformation and renewal is continuous because it is driven by the accelerating speed of change. Large organizations can no longer be slow to act and respond to shifts in their environment. Chapter 1 discusses the true challenge of transformation and provides a road map for making a transformation journey that will involve employees and enable them to support the new direction.

# I.

# Challenges of Organizational Transformation

An organization must address five challenges if it is to achieve significant change. This chapter discusses these challenges:

1. Role of a compelling direction or vision
2. Need for many elements to change
3. Identification of personal interests and turf protection
4. Exposure of deeply embedded culture, practices and assumptions
5. Role of the organization's size and need for speed to market

## Role of a Compelling Direction or Vision

One of the central roles for leadership is to articulate a vision for the organization that will serve as a beacon of light pointing to the organization's goal. The vision should be stable for a period of time. How long it remains viable is determined by the nature and stability of the organization's environment. Ideally, a vision statement should represent a challenge that motivates its members. It should be specific enough to enable all stakeholders to understand the business they are in, the direction they are going and the organization's goals.

The greatest example of a vision is the one articulated for the space program by President John F. Kennedy. His vision in 1961 was "to put a man on the moon by the end of the decade." At that time the United States was well behind what were perceived as superior Russian capabilities in the race to space. The vision represented a clear challenge. It was motivating and specific enough to direct action for all participants in the program. At the same time, it allowed all citizens to feel enormous pride and ownership when the goal was accomplished.

The difficulty of doing this at a corporate level is that the vision must fit all parts of the organization. For a large and diverse organization the resulting vision statement may be too generalized to be compelling or motivating. We have often heard complaints from employees who believe their corporate vision is inadequate to guide action or to motivate employees. We encourage them to define a vision for their part of the organization that is aligned with the corporate vision but provides direction and challenge for their work groups. This activity helps people understand just how challenging defining a vision can be. It also helps them to understand the role their part of the organization will play in achieving the corporation's visionary goals. During a period of great change, developing this understanding and being able to explain it to others is a critical step in the transformation.

A shared vision is critical to enabling employee empowerment. Management cannot create the vision in isolation, put it on parchment and hang it in offices throughout the company and expect employees to feel the ownership that comes through participation. To create a shared vision, people from throughout the company need to engage in dialogue about what the vision means to them and how they can make it operational on a daily basis. It becomes truly shared when employees begin making decisions on behalf of the customer based on the vision they are striving to achieve.

## Need for Many Elements to Change

In their book *The Art of Japanese Management: Applications for American Executives,* Richard T. Pasquale and Anthony G. Athos identified seven management tools that the Japanese and many U.S. companies use successfully to create an organization culture that is productive and effective. Figure 2 illustrates these tools in an interlocking framework; this is a useful model for understanding and guiding the transformation process.

The Seven S Framework is an integration model that includes *strategy, structure* and *systems,* which the authors describe as the *hard S's,* and *style, staffing, skills* and *shared*

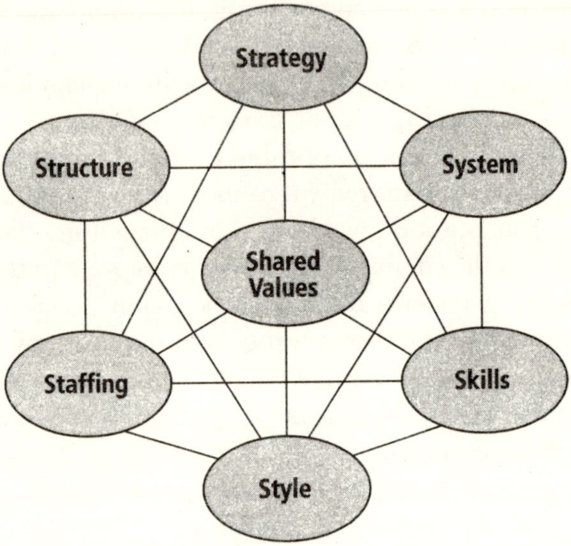


Source: Richard T. Pascale and Anthony G. Athos. *The Art of Japanese Management: Applications for American Executives*

***Figure 2. Seven S Framework***

*values,* which they describe as the *soft S's.* We have synthesized a definition of each of the S's as follows:

- *Strategy:* The way in which competitive advantage will be achieved.
- *Structure:* The way in which tasks and people are divided. The basic grouping of activities and reporting relationships. The primary basis for specializing and integration.
- *Systems:* Formal systems and procedures including management control systems, performance

measurement and reward systems, budgeting systems, information systems, planning systems and capital budgeting systems.

- *Style:* Leadership of top management and the overall operating style of the organization. Style reflects the norms people act on and how they work and interact with each other and with customers.
- *Staffing:* Employee selection and their backgrounds and competencies. Includes the approaches taken to recruitment, selection and socialization; how managers are developed; how young recruits are trained, socialized and integrated; and career management.
- *Skills:* Basic competencies that reside in the organization. Can be distinctive competencies of people, management practices, technology and so on.
- *Shared values:* Guiding concepts and fundamental ideas around which the company is built. Shared values focus attention and give purpose and meaning to the organization. Usually these values are simple and abstract and even seem trivial from the outside, but they have great meaning and guide behaviors within the company.

A high-performance organization has alignment (i.e., a constantly evolving fit) among all elements of the model. The elements are interdependent and function as a system. As change is introduced into any of the elements, there are implications for the others. Failure to consider all elements will create problems and unsatisfactory performance. To put an integrated plan into effect, managers must take a total systems approach to transformation.

The underlying premise of Pasquale and Athos's work is that U.S. executives tend to focus on the hard S areas. They noted that companies that are the highest performers in their industries revealed that their general managers paid far more attention to the softer elements than did their counterparts in less successful competitive firms. For example, leaders may concentrate their energy on strategy development accompanied by a change of structure to realign resources to match this new strategy. A systems change, such as reengineering, calls for a redesign of the workflow accompanied by a parallel redesign of the performance improvement tools (i.e., hardware and software) used by workers in the process. For these strategic or reengineering changes to be successful, management must look for accompanying changes in the soft S's.

The framework is useful as a road map during the visioning process and as a diagnostic tool during implementation. Managers begin by identifying the characteristics of the organization as it currently exists. Then they compare or contrast those characteristics against the characteristics that must support the new strategy. Following this road map makes it possible to describe the new organization's culture and to determine the extent of change that must occur during the transformation process.

Figure 3 shows an example of this comparison, based on the telecommunications industry before and after deregulation.

| **BEFORE:** | |
|---|---|
| Vision: | Universal service: low-cost telephone service for all; high penetration level |
| Strategy: | Local monopolies granted; full service providers for all customers; regulatory oversight; guaranteed return tied to interest rates. Business-subsidized residence; long-distance-subsidized local service |
| Structure: | State chartered, decentralized organizations; functionally organized |
| Systems: | Managed through standardized operating practices (industry-wide); technology standards agreed to and fully adopted; long life cycles for systems and capital investments |
| Style: | Autonomous, hierarchical, paternalistic; lifetime employment |
| Staffing: | 30% Management: college degree; trained for the industry; functional expertise developed and rewarded through promotions |
| | 70% Craft: high school graduate; trained for position; locally sourced as needed. |
| Skills: | Finance, legal, operations, management, technical, customer service |
| Shared values: | Reliability, equal access to service, affordability, community service, good employment, good employee benefits, lifetime career opportunities based on experience |

| **AFTER:** | |
|---|---|
| Vision: | Information superhighway |
| Strategy: | Open local exchanges to competition; equal playing field for multiple competitors who will use a variety of approaches to build a new communications infrastructure and many new services for the public; open competition will keep rates affordable |
| Structure: | Global consortiums form for specific market purposes; organization structures become flexible, permitting resources to be reallocated to meet emerging needs; consolidation within the industry is mirrored within organizations; organizations are formed around markets (rather than functions) |
| Systems: | Systems are increasingly important as performance enhancement and productivity tools; much focus on process and process streamlining; much focus on core competencies and outsourcing the noncore activities to others who can accomplish these activities as their core competency |
| Style: | Consensus management; teaming; coaching for performance; empowerment |
| Staffing: | Hire specialized talent externally; use contractors wherever possible; carefully manage overhead through headcount targets |
| Skills: | New technology; software development; marketing; finance; legal |
| Shared values: | Market-focused services; profitable growth; customer service; value-based pricing; technical expertise; family-friendly practices; competitive compensation and benefits; external experience in competitive, consumer services organization |

***Figure 3. Telecommunications industry before and after deregulation***

The Seven S Framework for the telecommunications industry, essentially a regulated monopoly before competition was introduced in the mid 1980s, was well defined and implemented consistently throughout all of the telephone companies within the industry. Changes in technology or regulation were introduced slowly so that the goal of universal service would not be compromised. As regulation changed to permit competition in increasing portions of the business, the industry's culture changed profoundly. A review of Figure 3 indicates massive change that essentially reinvented an industry and all of the players in it. The process of deregulation began in the mid-1980s with long distance services and will continue to evolve for another decade as it is introduced into all segments of the local exchange networks.

Within our company, the Seven S Framework has been introduced to all management employees as part of their educational development. They have been asked to use it for diagnostic and planning purposes within their areas of operation as our organization evolves into a new, competitive model. Over the four years we have been working with this tool, we have seen a shift from the areas of strategy and systems to the areas of staffing and skills. This shift signals to us that we have achieved greater understanding and commitment to the company's overall direction. Managers are now focusing their energies on obtaining and keeping the right knowledge and skills for successful execution of the strategy.

Many elements must be changed during a transformation effort. However, we have found this framework a simple way to think about and organize change. It has enabled all of our managers to become involved, using a common analytical approach. It helps us define the overall culture required and the contribution needed from every part of the organization. This is an important step in maintaining a connection with people.

## Personal Interests and Turf Protection

This area is a major challenge for transformation efforts and can be found at all levels of the organization. Until people can understand "what's in this for me" and come to accept the new order of things, they will resist the change. Leaders need everyone behind them, in support of company goals. The challenge is to ensure that there is something in the new direction for all stakeholders. Leaders must be persuasive in communicating with all stakeholders so that they will support the needed changes. Many reengineering efforts failed to achieve the desired level of success because employees saw their future employment at risk. We did not achieve complete execution in our own experience. Focus groups of employees (primarily hourly and union workers) felt that management had given them a solution to be implemented rather than a problem to be solved. Because they had not been involved in defining the solution, they did not feel any particular ownership for the problem. Management had failed in persuading this stakeholder group of the need for change and then failed to involve them in contributing their ideas for how the change could be best accomplished. We had to close a significant gap with hourly and union employees in order to recreate a feeling of connection and ownership.

## Deeply Embedded Culture, Practices and Assumptions

If an organization has been relatively stable for several years, its culture, practices and assumptions are most likely deeply embedded. The telecommunications industry, for example, documented and shared practices among the industry as industry standards. This level of standardization allowed for consistent connectivity and similar experiences using the network, regardless of where the user was located. Assumptions are frequently not as explicitly stated and yet are the understood basis for decision making. During a time of change, it is important to get people into the habit of stating their assumptions and challenging those that do not fit with the new direction.

In our experience, we have found that some existing practices stand in the way of change. Also, we have needed to create new practices to support behaviors we wanted to encourage. For example, we did not have a successful method for encouraging new ideas from employees. Previous attempts at employee suggestion programs had not succeeded and had in fact left very negative and deeply held perceptions of what employees could achieve. We had to work to overcome both of these beliefs before significant progress could be achieved in building a comfort level between management and employees that would lead to increased involvement.

## Size of the Organization

The larger the organization, the harder it will be to achieve change and the longer it will take. If it is possible to work within smaller units simultaneously, the cycle of change can be reduced. Each unit of leadership must be a role model for change. Otherwise, employees will not believe that the change direction is sincere. They take their cues from their supervisors. Leaders have to provide supervisors with examples and tools so that they have the wherewithal to support and achieve company goals.

## Summary

This chapter began with the premise that all organizations need to be adaptable in order to achieve success and sustain it. The amount of change required depends on many external influences, such as the amount and aggressiveness of competition, the speed with which new technological breakthroughs affect the industry, changes in the regulatory framework governing the industry, and changes in customer preferences. Changing an organization inevitably involves reengineering both the hard S's of strategy, structure and systems and the underlying culture embodied in the soft S's of style, staffing, skills and shared values. Thus, change requires a holistic approach; all parts of the organization need to be aligned toward creating the infrastructure that will support the new direction.

The Seven S Framework is a useful tool to support the visioning process for the new organization's culture and as a diagnostic tool for taking the organization's pulse along the way. Chapter 2 provides a blueprint that was useful to us in finding ways to make the new direction and vision operational on a daily basis for employees.

# II.

# The Workforce Blueprint

ONCE THE ORGANIZATION has clearly defined and communicated its vision, it must determine the organizational and strategic competencies required to support the vision and strategic thrusts. We define the term competency to include the combination of knowledge, skills and attitude required for the organization's success or, at a personal level, for the individual employee's success. Does the organization currently have the required competencies? If not, can they be bought or developed? The outcome of this analysis could lead to a series of partnerships or acquisitions in order to attain the required capabilities.

Once the competencies have been determined, it is essential to work with all employees to build a shared sense of ownership around the corporate vision and culture. The Workforce Blueprint Model (see Figure 4) is a behavioral model that provides a logical view of how the organization responds in support of new marketplace drivers, a new organizational vision and a new set of strategic thrusts.

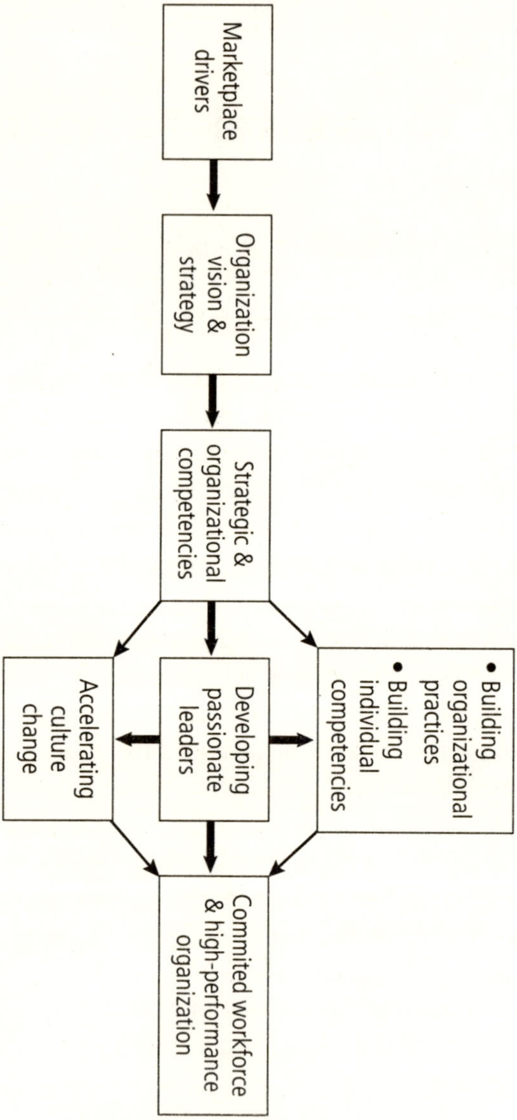


***Figure 4. Workforce Blueprint model***

To create this behavioral blueprint, the organization first designs an organizational competency model around the competencies necessary to support the vision. For example, if the vision is to provide the products and services that will win in the domestic and international marketplace and to differentiate the organization by service, then the organizational competency model might look something like this.

An organization characterized by:

- Superb marketing capability, domestic and international
- Customer-first mentality
- Speed to market
- Rapid movement of information across the organization
- Innovation and technological excellence
- Employer-of-choice status

The related Workforce Blueprint might look like this:

A workforce committed to

- Putting the customer above all else
- Speed in executing
- Action in spite of constraints
- High standards of accountability and responsibility
- High personal standards of performance

- Maintaining currency of skills
- Challenging the status quo
- Collaboration and teamwork
- Aggressively pursuing opportunities and customers globally

The final behavioral model might include five to ten submodels under which specific behavioral traits are identified for all levels of the organization.

The relevance of this work is that it defines the company "way" or "spirit." It is the way in which leaders lead and the workforce members in general relate to one another and work together to meet current and future challenges, no matter which division or line of business they represent. At the division or business unit level, other more technical competencies are identified and measured. It is like peeling the layers of an onion, always working to a more precise level of detail.

This Workforce Blueprint is the starting place for establishing a *competency-based framework*. Competency-based frameworks at the organization level describe the predominant characteristics required for success by that business unit, given its objectives and the competitive environment. At an individual level, the framework describes the breadth of knowledge, degree of skill, depth of experience and attitude required for success within an organization.

When creating these models, we have been successful working with small, cross-functional groups of employees from various levels of the organization. We facilitate thoughtful discussion around a series of questions about the behavioral model. These questions include:

- What behaviors, skills or knowledge areas will the new strategy require?
- Which strengths will we want to carry forward?
- What behaviors, skills or knowledge areas will we need to augment or strengthen?

The output of these work sessions can lead to constructive analysis of the best methods for filling identified gaps. It is an excellent early step in helping employees understand the personal changes required to achieve success for the organization.

The behavioral model is very clearly aligned with the organization's vision and corporate-wide business goals. The vision and the behavioral model provide the foundation for all supporting systems in the infrastructure. They give shape and purpose to the organization. Together they provide the business context for a deeper understanding of how day-to-day activities fit into the larger picture. Without this framework, no true employee empowerment can occur because there are no guiding principles supporting independent actions. With the framework, however, employees know what to do and how to do it–even when spans of control have been greatly increased and supervisors are not as accessible as in the past.

This framework helps to build strategically aligned organization practices in:

- Employee selection
- Succession planning

- Compensation
- Reward policies
- Leadership development and training
- Technical and customer service training
- Coaching and team skills training

These practices are important because they provide visible evidence that the company is committed to its stated business direction and behavioral values. For example, if a company espouses teamwork, compensation systems should provide team incentives, and all other people practices should also support the value of teamwork.

Additional support processes include:

- Work and family and diversity initiatives
- Employee suggestion tools
- Strategic employee communications
- Union involvement

Once this infrastructure is in place, there must be ways to measure success. In addition to customer feedback and financial performance measures, a system of metrics for people practices includes:

- Employee opinion surveys
- 360-degree feedback for leaders
- Team assessment tools
- Performance management systems

- Certification of skills and knowledge gained as a result of education and training

Individual competencies are also important to define. In one-on-one interviews, members of senior management across the corporation need to spell out the behavioral traits required for success. They should be encouraged to describe role models for all significant levels of the employee population. In our case, the various levels included frontline employees, first-line management, middle management, department heads or executive management, and senior management. Compiling the one-on-one interview data, we were able to extract a small set of *core competencies* that were critical to all employees, regardless of their role in the organization. Those competencies were leadership, market focus, continuous improvement and critical thinking.

At a level of detail below the competency description, we identified behavioral attributes that reflected the knowledge, skill or experience levels appropriate for the level of the employee population. This core competency model was integrated into the people practices identified previously so that we had a holistic approach to building competencies for individuals and a focus across the range of supporting processes and systems. This core competency model is illustrated in Figure 5.

In order to properly emphasize the need for specialized skills and knowledge, management must go beyond a definition of core competencies for particular functions and divisions of the business. For example, employees in the marketing or finance disciplines, those in customer contact

| | |
|---|---|
| **Continuous improvement** | Actively seeks to improve the quality and efficiency of work by constantly improving business knowledge, identifying improvements, driving for change and demonstrating urgency |
| **Customer focus** | Meets or exceeds customer expectations by anticipating and understanding customer needs, exhibiting flexibility, generating value-added solutions, taking personal responsibility and demonstrating business knowledge |
| **Leadership** | Gains support and confidence of others by asserting own ideas, listening and collaborating, driving for results, taking accountability, providing constructive feedback and building relationships |
| **Critical thinking** | Performs responsibilities of current role with professional excellence by generating "out-of-the-box" solutions and making sound decisions |

***Figure 5. A solid foundation: core competencies***

centers or those who work in highly technical positions will have additional behavioral attributes included in their expectations of performance. These attributes must be developed.

During a transformation effort, all people-supporting policies are aimed at establishing a new set of expectations and building passionate leaders for change at all levels of the organization. If successful, this effort will accelerate the culture change toward a committed workforce and a high-performance organization, as shown in the Workforce Blueprint (see Figure 4).

## Role of the Human Resources Organization

Much of the material presented in this book could be the work of a human resources (HR) organization. We hope it is also obvious that this work cannot be accomplished without strong and equal partnership with key business leaders throughout the organization. In fact, it falls upon the HR staff to interpret the business' objectives and strategic direction into those people-supporting practices that will enable employees to work at fulfilling the desired objectives. Following are some examples of how the partnership works:

- Education and training staff must work closely with business leaders to create educational experiences that accurately reflect the business drivers and internal knowledge and skill development priorities. Those experiences also must be offered to employees in a way that makes it easy for the participants. Factors such as time away from the job, travel expense, technological platforms for alternative delivery and budgetary constraints must be considered when designing, developing and delivering education. On the other side of the partnership, business leaders must come to appreciate the power of education to change knowledge, opinion and behavior and to use it as a strategic approach to change. This includes their personal involvement, interest and managing of the resource as an asset to be mined instead of an expense to be cut.

- Different segments of the HR community must cooperate continuously. It is only natural that each segment will have pet projects and want to favor them. Often different projects are aimed at similar objectives. Simplifying to the essential few projects saves resources and improves results.

  One of our most revealing undertakings was an inventory of the change initiatives in one of our business units. When each initiative was summarized on a single sheet of paper, there were enough initiatives under way to fill a two-inch binder! It was also evident that most of the initiatives were not achieving optimal results because they were deployed separately in "pockets." Through a collaborative team effort, we focused this business unit on a select few initiatives that had demonstrated success. This enabled us to create synergy among the programs and focus the messages consistently on the major themes. We also achieved full deployment of the selected initiatives across the business unit. This effort was helpful in eliminating the confusion that comes from multiple messages and multiple sources. We were also able to gain stronger emotional and financial support from business leaders for the remaining programs, as leaders were able to focus their time on the high-priority change initiatives.

- An example of partnering to overcome turf protection during change is fostering an environment where people can work collaboratively to achieve their objectives. There are many ways in which to do this, but generally someone or some function outside of the line organization needs to act as facilitator. A neutral party can see common interests and redundant work efforts more easily than those people closely involved with a project. Those closest to a project will often be more familiar with the points of difference in their project and therefore will be reluctant to compromise. A number of benchmark companies have used team-based action learning to bring people together in a neutral environment to address common problems and opportunities collaboratively. Out of these focused efforts has come an appreciation of the talents and capabilities of the team members and a voluntary continuation of collaboration for other initiatives.

- A final, but important example of building alliances, is the area of team composition. Tools for leadership development, such as the 360-degree survey instrument, help people see their strengths and weaknesses as others see them. This insight can be used to focus personal development on an ongoing basis. It can also be used to select a team that augments the leader's areas of weakness. Building a strong team with balanced capabilities is one of the fastest ways to become a high-performance organization.

## Tools for Change

In the rest of this chapter we focus on three effective tools for bringing about change at management levels. These tools are education, communication and rewards. Properly aligned, they are powerful accelerators for change.

### *Education*

Leaders feel frustrated when information suggests employees do not understand the company's direction or that employees do not trust management to do the right thing for stakeholders. These leaders will say, "I've been talking about this for a long time . . . don't they listen? Don't they see what is happening? Why don't they understand?" Based on our experience, we would argue that they do listen, they see a lot more than management generally thinks and they understand the discrepancies between the "talk" and the "walk." However, employees come at a business view from a different perspective. Quite often, that perspective is not visible to senior management for a variety of reasons.

Generally, we have found that senior management can easily become sheltered from the issues at the frontline or customer interface. In operational reviews, performance indicators are at a level that does not include this detail. Also, few forums exist for two-way dialogue with employees at all levels. Even when opportunities exist, employees are not comfortable raising business issues or concerns with senior management in public. They may be loyal to their supervisors and do not wish to compromise them in any way or simply may not know how to raise the issue. Those who are brave enough to do so typically do not speak the same language, meaning the same terminology, appropriate buzz words, and so forth, as senior management. Unfortunately, the message gets mixed up with the communication style of the messenger and is often dismissed, unless the executive is especially sensitive or has earlier frontline experience.

We have used the corporate education process as a deliberate strategy to overcome these inhibitors to effective communication throughout the organization. We created a core curriculum of programs that were designed to achieve two sets of objectives:

Objectives to Help the Corporation Succeed

- Develop an understanding of
  - Challenges of corporate transformation
  - Challenges and opportunities in the industry
  - Our corporate strategy
  - Our financial issues (how we will fund the opportunities)
  - The challenge of market leadership
- Develop assessments of
  - Our current state of market leadership
  - Our organizational strengths and weaknesses
- Develop ideas and action plans for
  - Our business units
  - Our personal development

Objectives to Help Employees Succeed
in the Future Corporation

- Develop an understanding of the core competencies required today:
    - Leadership
    - Market focus
    - Critical thinking
    - Continuous improvement
- Receive a competency assessment from peers and subordinates
- Practice using new knowledge and skills in a business simulation
- Develop personal developmental action plans and commitments

We created a core course for frontline employees, and for each of four levels of management, addressing both groups of objectives. Over a four-year period, all employees attended a session addressing the organization's strategies and key issues. The sessions were designed to focus appropriately on areas of concern given the employees' and managers' roles and scope of authority to take action. The model shown in Figure 6 illustrates the flow of the course, from the strategic and conceptual level to a level of personal leadership and accountability. Specifically, we wanted to motivate people to accept responsibility for change within the organization and for their own development.

These sessions ranged in length from four days to six and a half days. They were typically off-site programs so that participants could distance themselves from the demands of work and home while reflecting on the future of the business and their career aspirations. The sessions combined a variety of learning methods, including:

- Facilitator-led large group discussions
- Selected mix of participants for relevant discussions
- Small group discussions for teams

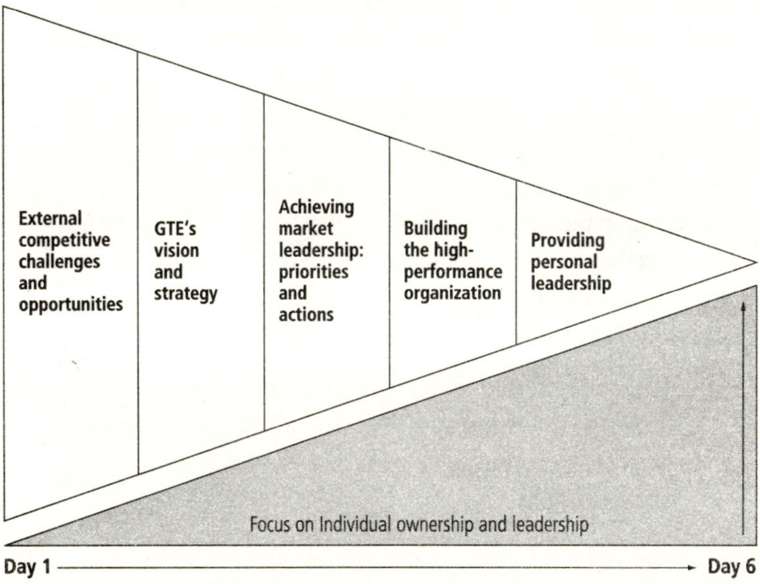


***Figure 6. Our approach to management development***

- Case studies
- Computer-based business simulations
- Discussions with senior management
- Assessments
- Action plans
- Public commitments of action

The facilitator guided the discussion so that real issues surfaced and could be discussed openly and thoroughly. The participants brought in differing perspectives to broaden the view. The facilitator permitted some time for venting but also guided the discussion to highlight opportunities for the participants to take responsibility and offered appropriate methods for bringing up important concerns with strategy. In addition, the major issues were shared with the affected part of the organization. Many of these issues found their way into the course content so that they provided additional learning opportunities for participants. In that way, the courses continuously reflecting the concerns and issues of employees and the organization.

The core curriculum had the following results:

- They deepened the understanding of the factors forcing the industry changes and how the corporation was preparing to win in a new and different environment.
- They pushed for personal responsibility and accountability, rather than permitting upwards finger-pointing.

- They uncovered possibilities for partnerships across the organization based on shared opportunities and similar problems.
- They pulled senior management to a different style of engagement with employees–from formal, scripted one-way presentations to informal, interactive, two-way dialogues.
- They increased the demand for education as employees became aware of the need to enhance their professional skills and as managers saw the power of the partnership with education to support the accomplishment of their objectives.
- They worked to bring alignment of purpose from frontline through senior management levels.

The original set of core courses was retired after the completion of the four-year cycle. A new set of core courses has replaced them, raising the bar on expectations of performance and benefit to participants.

The core curriculum strategy is most effective as a driver for change when it meets the following criteria:

- Senior management is actively involved in shaping the content and in some portion of the delivery process.
- Full deployment is achieved.
- The content stays current.
- The participation in each session is managed so that relevant issues can be brought up and discussed satisfactorily.

- Continuous improvement is evident to management and the participants.

### *Communication*

When you can share knowledge about a situation, that new understanding can lead to a change of perception and, ultimately, behavior. Affecting perception and changing behavior is the aim of a communication strategy. Unfortunately, communication strategies often seem to fall short of that objective, causing much frustration to those involved.

The role of communication is to provide (a) a steady stream of reinforcement for the organization's core beliefs and values, (b) information on achievements toward meeting the organization's goals and (c) information on new or changing actions, either internally or externally, that have an impact on the business direction. Many formalized methods are available for achieving communication. These are some of the traditional approaches:

- Senior management presentations, speeches and published articles or interviews
- Internal newspapers or bulletins
- External, public articles
- Advertising and promotional materials
- Management actions

These methods tend to be one-way-out, offering little opportunity in real time to know how the audience is receiving the message. Of course, it is possible with increasingly sophisticated methods to conduct surveys to measure the effect of a communication strategy and use the results to adapt the message going forward. Survey methodology today enables organizations to conduct sample polls on critical business issues and, much like national political polling techniques, attain feedback quickly to modify messages, thereby achieving better understanding.

One of the valuable benefits of instructor-facilitated education is the ability to form an instant assessment of how a message is being received by the audience, particularly if it is understood well enough to change behavior. If a misunderstanding is constraining the desired behavior change, that misunderstanding can be addressed immediately. Web-based communication networks also enable real-time audience feedback.

Tremendous power can be realized within a company when the major communication messages are linked to the company's educational and organization development processes. This allows the organization to have greater success in getting the level of understanding deep enough to drive for desired behavior change. The keys to a successful communication strategy are (a) alignment of messages to the overall business direction and (b) discipline to stay with a few critical themes and provide continuous reinforcement.

Our work with culture change over the years has led us to seek these linkages:

- Align business strategy to organization development, employee learning and communication initiatives.

- Enlist your senior team as change advocates and champions who are partners in organization development, learning and communications efforts.

## *Rewards*

Through communication, employees learn what is required; through education, they gain the knowledge and skills to do what is required; and through the reward system, they gain the motivation to do it. The third tool, the system of rewards available to managers to reinforce the desired outcomes, is powerful if used effectively. Conversely, if the system awards a conflicting set of behaviors, the results will be undermined significantly.

The area of rewards offers great opportunity for improvement in organizations. It does not matter whether the organization is in the public or private sector, for profit or nonprofit. Fundamentally, there are many ways to recognize achievement and to reward desired results in addition to financial compensation. Managers quite often are not creative enough in their approach, or they do not put adequate thought into aligning rewards to their objectives consistently throughout the organization.

We do not pretend to be experts in compensation systems; however, in our work with culture change initiatives, we can suggest some general guidelines:

- Support any effort at major change in the organization with appropriate rewards for achieving the desired outcomes. Change is not easy, and those who achieve it should be noticed for their effort.

We frequently observe change initiatives undertaken with no change in rewards.

- Make sure employees can be clear on the priorities. Often there are many objectives to achieve, distracting employees from the prime objective. The fewer the objectives, the better; but in any event, people should be clear on which are the critical few. It is amazing to see the sheer number of objectives for which people often are accountable.
- Actively work to eliminate rewards that are in conflict with desired results. This sounds obvious and easy, but it is not always evident at first. Sometimes these conflicts will surface as you begin to observe the unintended consequences of the change. When you analyze what is behind those unintended outcomes, you will often find a reward system that is out of sync with what you are trying to achieve. It may be in a part of the organization that you did not realize you were affecting. Be sensitive to this possibility.
- Be creative. Combine tangible rewards with the intangible rewards of recognition. If the reward is new, consider whether the reward itself needs a communication strategy. The following example described how this lesson was learned painfully as part of our culture change initiative.

Our employee opinion survey indicated that front-line, hourly employees did not feel a sense of ownership and accountability with the new business direction the organization was pursuing. This attitude was strikingly different from the perceptions of management employees. Our analysis led us to provide a form of tangible ownership to hourly employees in the form of stock options. Extending stock options to all hourly employees was a unique form of reward for a corporation of our size, and management believed they were offering a benefit that would be highly valued by employees and one that showed their commitment to the workforce. When the stock option plan was launched, the reaction was the complete opposite. Most employees did not understand the long-term value of stock options and how the stock could, over time, provide an important source of savings for them. Clearly, this reward required an education process so that people could see the value. Fortunately, management was committed to this process and followed the initial offering with another, larger one a year later. In addition, we have augmented this benefit with the opportunity for financial planning and advice for those who need to learn more.

# III.

# Choosing the Tools for the Tool Kit

The workforce blueprint is built on the premise that success in the marketplace is achieved ultimately by a committed and high-performing workforce with access to the right tools for the right job. These tools may be as tangible as the right hardware and software applications to facilitate the work or as intangible as a common set of assumptions and beliefs about organizational aspirations.

In the past, most organizations paid attention to the tangible tools, while largely ignoring the intangibles that could help align the workforce on goals critical to the future of the enterprise. Today, more companies recognize the need to ignite the passion and imagination of their employees if they are to successfully address greater market complexities and achieve organization transformations that meet their increasing challenges. They are doing so, first, by providing solid evidence that they value their people who will make the company vision a reality. This evidence may include giving employees a greater stake in company ownership, offering more generous stock options to all employees, implementing flexible workplace policies and practices that recognize the needs of a diverse work-force, or making available a wider array of educational and developmental opportunities.

In addition, such companies increasingly are using a new set of learning tools with certain shared characteristics:

- Positive and future-oriented
- Cooperative and collaborative
- Energizing, creative and fun
- Revolutionary in spirit
- Nurtured at the grassroots

These characteristics are in part a required antidote to the demoralization and cynicism left in the wake of a decade or more of downsizing. These learning tools are sustainable in organizations whose leaders believe in their value and who share in the enthusiasm they can generate.

Two such powerful learning tools are *Appreciative Inquiry* and *Breakthrough Thinking.* Both tools are suited to organizations that are being re-created as a result of massive technological, market and internal change.

## Appreciative Inquiry

Appreciative Inquiry (AI) was brought to American management by Suresh Srivastva and David Cooperrider of Case Western Reserve University[1]. AI is an organization development approach that seeks the best of "what is" in organizations and then leverages the collective energy and confidence this form of investigation engenders to create a vision of "what might be." An appreciative inquiry begins by asking, What is it about the organization that gives it life, that has made success in the past a reality and will make success in the future possible?

Unlike the traditional problem-solving model of organization change, the underlying assumption of Appreciative Inquiry is that organizations offer employees solutions to discover and embrace collectively, rather than problems to uncover, isolate and solve independent of the whole system. Tradi-tional problem solving tends to concentrate on the status quo by focusing on problems that must be isolated and removed. Appreciative Inquiry promotes the creative impulse, fostering hope for the future and seeking to bring about the possible.

Appreciative Inquiry has four primary steps:

1. Discovering and valuing what gives life to organizations
2. Envisioning the future that is possible
3. Engaging in dialogue about possibility and creating a collective vision
4. Constructing the future through innovation and action

The steps of Appreciative Inquiry are usually introduced through the *4D Cycle,* which is presented as an alternative to problem solving (see Figure 7).

Applying the 4D Cycle takes the organization from initial valuing of the past and present to envisioning a

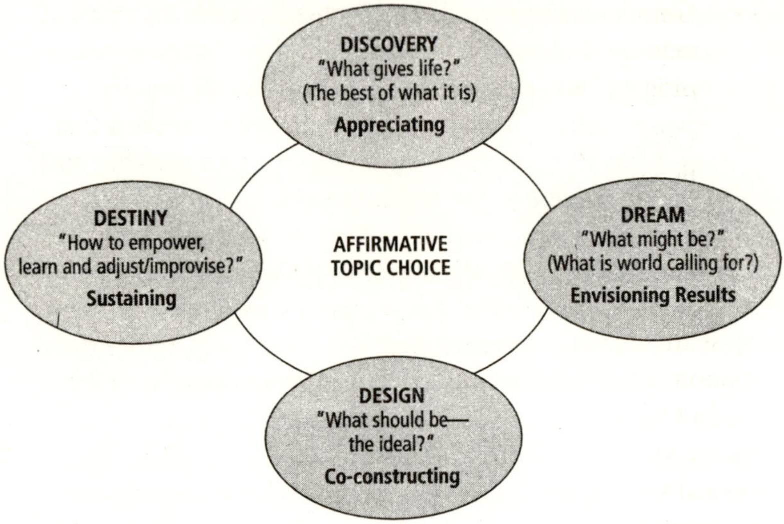


Source: David Cooperrider, 1996.

***Figure 7. 4D cycle***

more valued and vital future, creating the foundation of the envisioned future and delivering the envisioned future state.

The long-term goal of Appreciative Inquiry in organizations is to accelerate the development of four competencies, which were first defined by Frank Barrett[2].

- *Affirmative competence:* The ability to appreciate positive possibilities by focusing on current and past strengths and successes.
- *Expansive competence:* The ability to grow in new directions beyond what was previously thought possible.

- *Generative competence:* The ability collectively to create new systems and to contribute to the organization's progress and development.
- *Collaborative competence:* The ability to create collectively through ongoing dialogue and the exchange of diverse points of view.

Appreciative Inquiry can be applied in organizations in multiple ways–in workshops, in team-building sessions or as the foundation of a wide-scale organization transformation initiative. As in all change interventions, the scattershot approach yields little in the way of results. As a major tool in a carefully crafted change effort tied to the overall workforce blueprint, Appreciative Inquiry builds momentum for achieving long-term goals. It is particularly effective as the foundation of a grassroots movement for positive change among frontline employees in organizations with a deep understanding of the customer-service value chain. An example is described in Chapter 5.

## Breakthrough Thinking

Similar to Appreciative Inquiry, Breakthrough Thinking is future oriented and is applicable in organizations looking for tangible ways to break from the past in order to meet new business challenges. Like Appreciative Inquiry, Breakthrough Thinking builds on the understanding that simply doing more of the same things will not bring about new solutions. Both tools subscribe to the constructionist principle that we create models of the world through our thought processes, and thus, to change the models we must change our thinking.

The difference between the tools is primarily in their applications. Appreciative Inquiry lends itself to wide-scale organization transformation based on a series of interviews from throughout the company built on specific interview protocols. Breakthrough Thinking is best applied with teams focused on achieving hard, tangible results directed at specific business measures. Although rooted in deep philosophic thinking, Breakthrough Thinking can and has been used by sales teams looking to surpass previously set profit goals, for example, by significant (almost unrealistic) percentages. On other fronts, it has been used where teams of hourly workers looking for ways to improve work processes, kept work within the company that might have been outsourced, and thereby preserved jobs. In each of these examples, Breakthrough Thinking has been used to make significant differences to the bottom line, while also using new skills and techniques designed to help teams do several key things differently:

- Define issues based on future desired outcomes, rather than on making incremental improvements to existing business models
- Discover and use new ways of reaching goals and creating business solutions
- Develop and use new communication skills designed to create breakthrough results

Numerous consulting firms today offer breakthrough tools by proclaiming their ability to make participants in workshops and seminars "think outside the box." Although there is some merit to generic applications, the real benefit is derived from applying the techniques and skills to real-time business issues.

Breakthrough Thinking has its roots in the works of Donald Schon and Chris Argyris (theorists of "Action Science") and Peter Senge, among others. The culmination of the philosophic underpinnings for Breakthrough Thinking is found in Senge's book *The Fifth Discipline* and in *The Fifth Discipline Fieldbook,* edited by Senge and others.

In *The Fifth Discipline,* Senge describes ways in which our actions create our reality[3]. He goes on to demonstrate ways in which it is possible to change our reality by changing our behavior. Of the five disciplines described by Senge (systems thinking, personal mastery, mental models, building shared vision and team learning), the two disciplines most applicable to achieving breakthrough results are mental models and team learning. Both disciplines get to the heart of how we perceive reality and how we accordingly act on these perceptions. Breakthrough Thinking begins by posing the traditional problem-solving model and then presenting its counterpoint, the Breakthrough Model.

The traditional model follows a linear sequence of events, often using untested assumptions, and leads to incremental improvements at best (see Figure 8). It is a product of the mechanistic world view, more analytic than holistic.

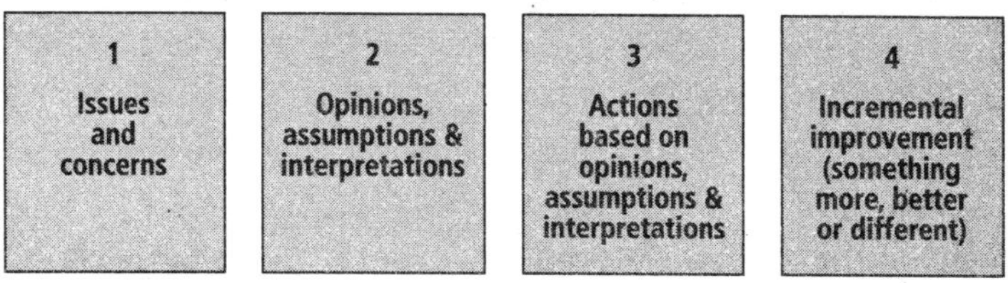


***Figure 8. Traditional management process***

In contrast, the Breakthrough Model (see Figure 9) depicts a process that begins with a clean slate. It describes a possibility and creates a community of commitment for achieving the possibility.

Inherent in the process is the belief that breakthroughs are possible when teams work together, through a rigorous process of shared vision, to shape a new reality. The rigor is in the discipline required to test assumptions and deeply held convictions together in order to achieve a new, commonly held belief in the breakthrough possibility and to arrive at a commonly held commitment to achieve it.

A breakthrough is described as the creation of an unpredictable, discontinuous result and a strikingly

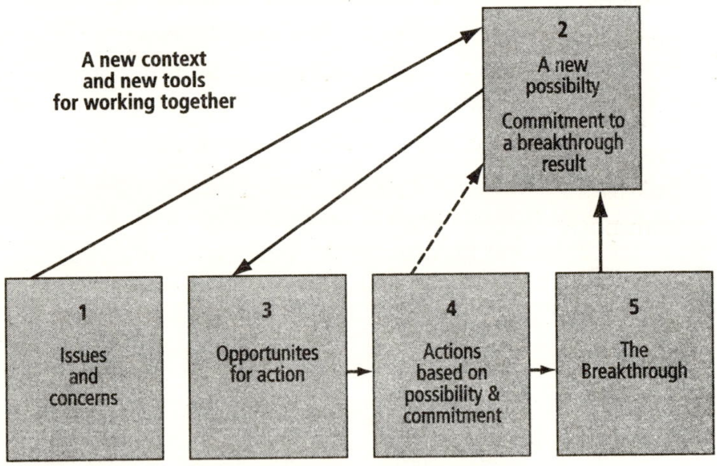


*Figure 9. The Breakthrough model*

important advance or discovery. A breakthrough has the following characteristics:

- Unprecedented
- Unpredictable
- Discontinuous from the past
- An interruption in the status quo
- Built on leadership
- Creates the future
- Out of the ordinary

The essential building block for breakthrough is *dialogue,* a rigorous discipline of listening for possibility and of advocating for positions only when underlying assumptions have been openly and honestly tested. The skills are personal but are played out in team settings.

Additional tools that foster employee commitment target the front line, often involving bargaining unit employees, who are increasingly recognized as the vital link to the customer. These frontline initiatives share common elements:

- They treat hourly employees as partners in the business, drawing on their expertise to create and implement solutions to business issues and to serve the customer.
- They are locally grown and managed, putting the emphasis on creating solutions that are close to the customer.

- They begin with thorough grounding in such techniques as team skills training, Appreciative Inquiry, and Breakthrough Thinking. Several such initiatives (e.g., Jumpstarters, Labor Optimization (using Breakthrough Thinking ), and Employee Zealots (using Appreciative Inquiry) are described in Chapter 5.

*Continuous process improvement,* another employee engagement tool, is a value that is embedded within the organization. It began with the quality improvement efforts launched in the mid-1980s and gained momentum with the process reengineering experiences of the early 1990s. When employees have a solid understanding of the core work processes vital to an organization, they are better able to understand their importance to the enterprises' success. For example, in our organization, the core processes include:

- Order entry
- Service order fulfillment
- Service assurance
- Billing

These core processes are supported by internal processes which include, for example:

- Product development
- Advertising and promotion
- Staffing
- Workforce development

Viewing the work environment from a process perspective is like putting on a special pair of lenses that enables one to see workflows that were previously hidden from view, for example:

- The relationships between parts of the organization
- Where the value to the end user is added
- Where the redundancy exists
- Where bottlenecks occur
- Where complexity or exceptions exist
- Where time gets added to the cycle of completion

When people learn how their actions affect others downstream in the process, they have a far greater sensitivity to respond with speed and accuracy than before. Their insights can then be organized into a *process map*.

Process maps are valuable tools for training employees. The methodology for developing the maps is also important to understand and is very easy to learn. As "disconnects" in the process are identified, they become the focal point for process improvement efforts by a selected team. Employees find this is a very gratifying effort.

As continuous process improvement becomes an established way of daily work, the ability of an organization to standardize a process flow is enhanced. This is important because the systems required to support the process can also be standardized, which leads to enormous cost savings for the organization.

Appreciative Inquiry and Breakthrough Thinking are valuable tools in the tool kit used to create a competitive workforce in the continuous improvement effort (see Figure 10).

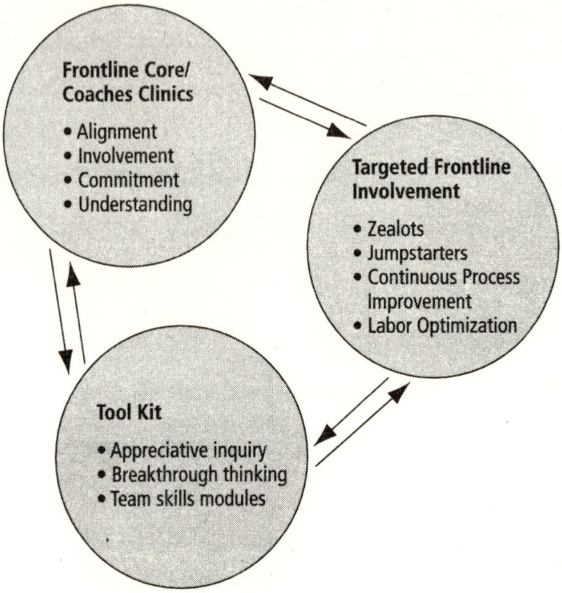


***Figure 10. Creating a competitive workforce***

# IV.

# Creating and Sustaining Organizational Learning

Cultures survive because they adapt to changes in their environment. They thrive when they can anticipate change or create change that is favorable to their strengths. Up to this point, we have discussed methods to connect employees to management's goals and objectives (i.e., to get agreement and alignment) and methods and tools to stimulate employee innovation in the creation of new ideas and progress toward those goals and objectives. In this chapter, we discuss how to create and sustain learning within the organization so that its members will continue to be curious, adaptable to new ideas and excited about embracing change and expanding in new directions.

Throughout this book, we have contended that truly innovative leaders today are paying serious attention to the people side of the business. They are ever aware that although you can acquire process expertise or technology, the one thing you cannot buy is employee commitment. Yet this may be the make-or-break advantage as change continues to accelerate in the marketplace of the twenty-first century. At the end of the day, it's "our" people against "their" people in the competitive marketplace.

Businesses today have to be flexible learning organizations, able to mobilize teams whose members know how to function quickly and efficiently across geographic and organizational boundaries. The tools and techniques of organizational learning and of teaming are key to business transformation.

## Background Note on Learning Organizations

The author credited with putting the term *learning organization* into everyday use is Peter Senge. His work, *The Fifth Discipline,* published in 1990, struck a chord that still reverberates in corporate America. He captured the attention of many readers who, unfortunately, were able to answer yes to the question that is the title of his book's second chapter: "Does your organization have a learning disability?" The antidote to the malady is found in Senge's schema of five disciplines: systems thinking, personal mastery, mental models, shared vision and team learning.

Senge defines the learning organization as one that continuously expands its capacity to create its future—where its people continuously learn how to learn together.

Other theorists have called for a more concrete definition, offering more emphasis on application. David A. Garvin suggests that a learning organization is skilled at creating, acquiring and transferring knowledge[4]. His five-part skill set for the learning organization includes systematic problem-solving, experimentation, learning from experience and past history, learning from the experience and best practices of others and transferring knowledge quickly and efficiently.

The common thread among many learning organization theorists, including Senge, Garvin, Chris Argyris, and Donald Schon, is that true organizational learning leads to a rigorous questioning process. This process produces insight that can be captured and transferred, and it is what ultimately changes behavior.

Asking people to think of an example of a learning organization invariably brings forth the model of an athletic team. A well-coached team is a balanced make-up of highly-skilled and talented members who have practiced their individual performances to become a disciplined whole. Goals are clear and easily understood by all. The rules of the game are also clear and fully understood by all participants.

These athletes devote considerable time on a regular basis to reviewing video tapes of previous performances, seeking opportunities to learn and improve their play. They practice their individual and team-based skills. They use scouts to observe their competitors in order to learn about the strengths and weaknesses of the opposing team members. They use this insight to establish so-called match-ups, attempting to use their strengths to their best advantage.

Continuing this analogy, the professional teams will also have a minor league system for ongoing development of young talent. This system provides depth to the organization. Team members are able to measure their progress and contribution easily by maintaining a record of relevant statistics on individual and team performance. Comparable benchmark data is easily available from neutral sources such as the news media. Feedback is immediate. Successes are celebrated, and mistakes are handled quickly, with an immediate ability to make changes in a game plan or the lineup in response to changing conditions. Being a member of a winning team feels great. Performance of all players tends to rise to a higher level. News commentators use the phrases, "They have elevated their play" or "They have picked the game up" to describe the emotional response to positive play.

In contrast, being a member of a team that is underperforming its potential is frustrating to its members. Frequently, team members will take more risks and make more mistakes in the process, acting out of desperation. Ultimately, they attempt to blame the team's performance on some of the members. This "blame game" undermines the team's morale. If unchecked, it will change the team make-up as the blamed members are forced out. So, it appears evident that a high-performance team becomes more than a sum of its parts. Success breeds a success momentum.

## Characteristics of a Learning Organization

The athletic team analogy allows people to visualize the characteristics of high-performance teams. The challenge is trying to duplicate these characteristics in a business environment, specifically in learning organizations. These are some of the characteristics a high-performance learning organization should have:

- Clear goals and objectives, understood by all members
- The ability to rapidly communicate and understand the game plan
- The ability to rapidly communicate and adjust to changes required by the competition
- A knowledge of the capabilities of members so that those human assets can be used to greatest advantage
- A coaching system to continuously develop the members of the team in a focused way
- A systematic way of learning from experience and sharing the lessons rapidly with other members
- An environment that fosters and encourages continuous learning and development of its members
- Management processes and systems that facilitate the sharing of relevant information and learning
- A systematic way of acquiring and developing new, talented members

This is a daunting list. There are many reasons why business organizations find it difficult to adapt the sports team analogy to their environment. Probably the greatest challenge is that few, if any, business organizations have such a singular focus on the optimization of human talent to achieve their goals.

One organization has achieved significant progress in becoming a learning organization: the U.S. Army. The Army has achieved a large-scale transformation through learning. Communications and learning technologies will continue to play a major role in improving each member's performance on the job by delivering intelligence to the individual at the place of work, even on the battlefield. The model of a learning organization developed by the Army is one that can apply to any organization, even those with less complex demands than the Army.

Some of the central tenets to adopt are:

- Leadership development at all levels of the organization
- Simulation–practice, practice, practice, before the bullets are real
- Learning laboratory and decision support tools
- Center for Lessons Learned
- Artificial intelligence
- After-Action Review process–no rank
- Best skills will win over rank
- Communication of strategic intent–let field officers determine tactics

The Army's methods and its results have been a major influence on us in our own attempts to transform an organization. We have adopted many of these central tenets in our efforts at transformation. Two of these tenets, leadership development and the role of education, are of particular interest.

## Leadership Development

The emphasis on leadership development has grown tremendously as an outcome of centralization, process reengineering and downsizing. As a decentralized organization there were many opportunities to build and practice leadership skills in positions of varying levels of responsibility–branch offices, district offices, division offices, headquarters, subsidiaries and so forth. Many of these broad, generalist jobs have been eliminated. It might appear that because there are fewer positions of broad leadership in the organization, the demand for leadership development would be reduced. However, specialist positions grew up in their places. The responsibilities are more narrowly focused and require deeper knowledge and skill. We find that, as people become more specialized, they feel less responsibility and ownership for overall business outcomes. It is not always clear to them how their efforts fit into or affect the overall plans. Employees often point their fingers upward to those who determine strategy and policy, rather than to themselves as those responsible for determining tactics and successful implementation in the marketplace. Adding to the problem, their performance measures are numerous and often are not clearly linked to overall goals and objectives–they too are more narrowly focused.

We have found that education is a critical vehicle to build understanding and to drive the behavioral change required. As employees build understanding of the nature and amount of change required to achieve objectives, they are uncovering the obstacles to change and taking steps to eliminate them.

## Role of Education

The primary goal of our mandated education is to focus all employees on the overall game plan for winning in the targeted markets and customer segments. Our education process has three phases: preparation, classroom experience and sharing the lessons learned. We work first at building a deep understanding of the plan, or in the Army's terms, the strategic intent. We then work at involving employees as they develop their plan of action in attaining specific objectives integral to the overall goals.

The first phase is preparation. Before attending a classroom experience, participants are required to complete assignments electronically using the company Intranet. These assignments include information gathering from a selected list of internal Web sites. Participants respond to questions regarding their organization's competitive readiness and receive multi-rater feedback on their personal performance in the company-selected core competencies. The goal of this phase is to begin the learning process on the Intranet, familiarizing them with what is available. The organization assessment outcomes also provide a focus for the in-class learning. The personal feedback provides a focus for development and a desire to change.

The second phase is a classroom experience. As part of this experience, individuals participate in a learning laboratory, which is a computer-supported model or simulation of our business. They work with their team members in running the business, striving to accomplish and balance the many objectives and competing demands they deal with in real life. The learning laboratory provides practice in a safe environment and allows participants to better understand the overall dynamics of the business. They gain a real perspective on the challenges of leadership.

At the conclusion of the learning laboratory, we conduct After-Action Reviews (AARs), another process borrowed from the Army. AARs provide employees with a framework or methodology for assessing the effectiveness of planned activities. The process seeks answers to three basic questions:

1. What was expected to happen?
2. What actually happened?
3. What would you do differently?

In completing the AAR the focus is on developing the data around the outcomes achieved so that people can gain insight into cause and effect. The AAR contributes to building a continuous learning process without the blame game. At the same time, we strive to build ownership and responsibility for actions.

During the classroom experience, each participant builds a personal plan of action. This plan is posted online for ease of sharing with the individual's supervisor.

This allows for supervisory coaching in support of the plan, which is part of the third phase.

In the third phase, the learning process is taken beyond the classroom and into the work site in a number of ways. The individual makes a commitment to complete a personal plan of action. We can follow up periodically, by using e-mail messages over the Intranet. We also conduct an AAR process for each of the action plans approximately three months after the classroom experience.

The final challenge is how to share the insights and lessons learned through experience so that others can get the benefit quickly, avoiding their own experience curve. In a large, geographically dispersed organization, we have frequently observed "pockets of excellence" where people are achieving outstanding results. If their approaches could be fully deployed across the entire organization, the benefit would be enormous. We have struggled with achieving full deployment. In the past, the primary reason for not achieving full deployment was the lack of information and an easy way to learn and share outcomes. The Army's concept of a Center for Lessons Learned appeared to be a real breakthrough on this issue.

We have adopted the Army's idea and inaugurated it with the launch of the mandated education process. By doing so, we assure that employees will contribute to the building of the knowledge base and also that they know of its existence and how to use it. Some of the results of the personal plans of action are entered into our Center for Lessons Learned database so that the results can be shared across the organization. The Center for Lessons

Learned is accessible to all employees. Lessons are categorized by relevant communities of practice or interest and can be sorted easily by key word.

Through this education process, we are also pulling people into the use of the Intranet as a tool for continual learning and knowledge building. Once we create this habit, we can more extensively use the network and individuals' work stations for other forms of education, knowledge creation and sharing.

# V.

# Application: A Case Study in the Telecommunications Industry

THE TELECOMMUNICATIONS INDUSTRY has changed dramatically since the early 1980s when the Bell system was broken up and the field was opened up for greater competition and choice. The regional Bell operating companies and the independents have been gearing up for comprehensive, domestic competition. Added to this picture are the growth of the global economy, massive technological changes, volatile market conditions, increasingly sophisticated customer demands and uncertainties in the regulatory arena. The industry's landscape has undergone a major transformation during the past few years alone.

During this same period, one telecommunications company–GTE–weathered all these changes and more. Soon after the Bell break-up, GTE began a series of reorganizations to gain more leverage and power from what had been a string of loosely connected independent phone companies. By the mid-1990s, after several consolidations and the largest telecommunications merger in U.S. history, GTE's telephone operations group became the nation's largest local exchange company. As part of its changing structure, it centralized and reengineered its core processes. The reengineering would improve efficiencies through such activities as work center consolidations and deployment of new systems. The result would be added value for the customer and reduced costs to make GTE more competitive. Employees had been told throughout the process that workforce reductions would result from these efforts, but by 1994, it was clear that downsizing was taking its toll on employee morale, especially among hourly workers, and that future productivity was being threatened.

## Background to the Culture Initiative

Ironically, it was also during this time that the first phase of a culture change effort was yielding strong, positive results among GTE's management ranks. By all measures (annual employee surveys and periodic communication polls), this group had a greater understanding of and commitment to the company's new vision, business direction, and strategy than at any other time over the previous five years, when the numbers had begun a serious decline.

This culture change had been accomplished through the Management Development Core experience, a series of courses designed for all levels of the company's management employees; through major communication initiatives, enlisting the company's senior and mid-level managers in sharing the company vision and direction down through the organization's management ranks; and through a redesign of the annual senior team conferences around leadership development rather than presentations and golf.

The second phase of what was to become known as the Culture Change Initiative was designed to reconnect with the front line after downsizing. This initiative could be realized only after the senior team had engaged in its own leadership development and team learning.

By February, 1996, the results of the annual employee survey were shared with GTE executives during their conference. According to the survey, management results were up in six of nine categories, nonexempt employee results were up in seven. In contrast, hourly employee results continued their disturbing trend, showing improvement in only two categories, while remaining flat or dropping in the other seven categories. The senior management team was in agreement that this situation could not stand. The hourly employees in Telephone Operations served more than 90 percent of GTE's customers. The stage was set to put in motion a plan for transformation, the goal–to ensure a connected, committed and passionate frontline workforce that was knowledgeable about the business, by focusing resources on the front line.

After a period of intensive listening, a Culture Council was formed to address the issues that had surfaced repeatedly in various employee groups and from formal survey data. The major areas of concern were:

- Sharing strategic business information
- Facilitating active frontline involvement
- Demonstrating leadership commitment–primarily in the form of investment in the front line
- Demonstrating commitment to the goals of the organization
- Rewarding achievement

The plan that was ultimately developed by the Culture Council, approved and subsequently funded addressed the issues in three significant ways:

- Creating targeted frontline training
- Creating a critical mass for change through a group of specially trained change agents–largely from the front line
- Providing stock options at all levels of the organization, including hourly (mostly unionized) employees

In addition, the employee survey process was redesigned to allow for timely reporting, with the understanding that employee measures would be shared regularly, along with financial and customer data. These results were to be viewed as equally important when looking at the indices of how the business was run. The common thread running through the culture initiative was Appreciative Inquiry.

## Targeted Involvement Initiatives

Two key principles learned from hourly employees on the advisory panel guided the development of the Targeted Involvement Initiatives:

- Give employees business issues to solve rather than solutions to implement
- Employees can and will solve business issues when they are treated like business partners

Embedded in each of these principles is the need to be heard, respected and brought to the table as an equal. The Targeted Involvement Initiatives started with the premise that no one knows the job better than the front-line employee who does the job and serves the customer every day. From providing forums for involving hourly employees in the day-to-day improvements in how the business was run to enabling them to implement break-through ideas, the Targeted Involvement Initiatives reflected this premise.

### *Labor Optimization*

An early example of a targeted frontline initiative was Labor Optimization, which made extensive use of Breakthrough Thinking (described in Chapter 3). Labor Optimization was successful from its inception because it built on a partnership with the unions. The mission of the initiative, jointly embraced by the unions and management, was to unite in efforts to develop and test innovative ideas that would lower labor costs to "equal to or less than a competitor's" while maintaining superior quality. Labor Optimization was designed to save jobs by engaging the field operations employees in efforts to keep the work inside rather than using contractors. The Labor Optimization effort used a steering committee, comprised of union and management employees, and was backed by the local union leadership and regional management. These teams, trained in Breakthrough Thinking, created and implemented the ideas that met the initiative's goals and kept work from being outsourced. Labor Optimization was successful in most of the regions where it was implemented, but it did not flourish in regions where union-management relations were not strong.

### *Jumpstarters*

Another initiative that thrived in regions with strong union-management relations was Jumpstarters. This initiative involved an external consultant who worked with local management to begin the process. The consultant facilitated the early team sessions by drawing out the issues and concerns of employees and allowing for necessary venting but also by setting action-oriented expectations. After issues were identified and prioritized, the consultant helped the teams to determine which issues could be resolved locally and which would have to involve other teams for resolution. This was an important distinction and contributed to a deeper understanding of how decisions in one area could have strong implications for other processes downstream. The team leader played a crucial role in involving other teams, handing off issues appropriately or in engaging his or her team in actively addressing the identified issues. Continued team action included team skills training directly related to the issues the team was tackling. For example, if scheduling, planning and prioritizing future work team efforts was critical, then a module in facilitating team meetings would be initiated. If conflict between or among teams was an issue, then a module in managing conflict would come into play. The main idea was to include team training on a just-in-time basis. The first session, led by the external consultant, however, was critical to ongoing success.

In summary, the first Jumpstarters session involved the following practices:

- Engaging the people who wanted to become involved–voluntary participation
- Listening to issues and concerns from the employees' perspective
- Facilitation of discussion to permit "airing" but avoiding "griping"
- Recording the issues
- Prioritizing the issues
- Separating issues with broader implications from local issues
- Initiating action on local issues
- Escalating the priority issues to senior management

Jumpstarter team involvement was often the hourly employees' introduction to continuous process improvement activities and teams. Issues identified by Jumpstarter teams had the potential of becoming a "feed" to the continuous process improvement teams aligned with GTE's core business processes.

Learning and adopting a process orientation extended the life of the Process Reengineering Program Management Office at GTE. After the core processes were implemented, the organization had to learn ways in which processes are kept new and refreshed as technology and market demands dictate. The role of the office shifted from development and implementation to continuous improvement. It enhanced and automated tools such as process mapping. Project management became a professional discipline adopted throughout the organization. More of GTE's technology units embraced International Standards Organization (ISO) certification. At the heart of each of these efforts was a renewed appreciation for involved and committed work teams. They acted with a vision and direction to follow and with the authority to be heard and to make a difference.

### *Coaches Clinics*

Another important initiative designed to enhance employee skill sets was Coaches Clinics. These were biannual sessions to provide first-line supervisors the support they need to better serve their frontline employees. The purpose was to create a forum for information sharing, solutions creation, and teaming among first-line supervisors and executive leaders. The desired outcome included an enhanced understanding of the strategic direction of the business, of market leadership initiatives and of new products and services, as well as a deeper knowledge of critical coaching skills. The Coaches Clinics were a key to ensuring that first-line coaches had the necessary information and skills to lead their teams of hourly employees.

To ensure that hourly employees were knowledgeable about the business, a training course called The Front Line Core Course was developed that would be delivered to every hourly employee twice a year. It would enable the frontline employees to learn the latest competitive and industry developments firsthand. Dialogue with local leaders was part of the program for a two-way information exchange. Course facilitators were recruited from the ranks of second-level supervisors, who received training in facilitation skills, course content and Appreciative Inquiry. Each segment of the core course was built on the principles of Appreciative Inquiry, to let employees learn applications relevant to themselves, their work teams and customers. These sessions involved training approximately 55,000 employees twice a year. They were widely viewed as critical to the business. GTE's telephone operations president was the initiative's key champion. He became personally involved in each session's design and content and provided videotaped messages for each new session as it was rolled out.

## *Employee Zealots*

An early application of Appreciative Inquiry involved an advanced group of specially trained change agents. By creating a criteria list for what were initially termed Employee Zealots (and later called the Positive

Change Network), the Culture Council enlisted the regions' operations and sales groups and the headquarters staff heads to nominate the first class of Zealots. This leading-edge class of thirty-four participants, representing all levels of the organization and including hourly, union employees, formed the pilot group. They were invited to the telephone operations headquarters, had dinner with the president and senior leaders, met the Culture Council and in the session itself entered into comprehensive and candid dialogue with the senior leaders. This set the stage for the training to come. The participants were immersed in two days of Appreciative Inquiry principles and applications. They generated key topic choices for interviews, determined actions they were going to take back home and presented their key ideas and insights to the senior leaders on the last day. The enthusiasm and excitement generated by the session led to an expansion of the program over the next several months.

The next session was broadened to include fifty-two zealots. By the third session, with close to ninety Zealots already trained, the scope was enlarged to bring together via satellite three sites across the country–the West Coast, the Midwest and headquarters on the East Coast. The basic format was the same, but the sense of being a part of a social movement was greatly enhanced. The key messages of confidence in the future, business growth and limitless opportunity–combined with the power of motivation and enthusiasm–reached a level of intensity previously untapped in cross-representational groups of employees.

The role of the Zealots was to create a wave of enthusiasm about the future of the company–about its role as a market leader in the telecommunications industry. The Zealots went back to their work locations and held employee meetings, some with two hundred or more employees. They applied Appreciative Inquiry in their own work groups and with customers. They networked with each other over the company Intranet, created a Web page and shared their stories of success across the various regions of the company. They conducted interviews on key topic choices identified as critical to the company's future success and contributed to a growing database of success stories to be shared across the company. The Zealots initiative tested assumptions about organization development change efforts. Although the telephone operations executives were instrumental in clearing a path for the Zealots, the employees themselves embraced the principles of Appreciative Inquiry. They began a grassroots movement for change unlike any other in the company's history.

## Results of the Culture Initiative

Soon after the culture initiative's full implementation, the telephone operations group was dramatically reorganized into three separate business entities–the network organization, the competitive deregulated business and the integrator organization. The integrator organization spanned all of GTE's businesses, including its nonwireline units. The strategy continues to be bundled service and product offerings, designed to make GTE the industry leader. The changes continue to be dramatic.

By the time of the massive reorganization, the results from the culture initiative were encouraging. Initiative evaluations were in the good-to-excellent range, indicating employee approval. The employee survey measures were showing a 3- to 5-percentage point increase in most topic areas, in spite of continuing change. All indicators suggested that the messages were getting down to lower levels of the organization, with significant increases in knowledge and understanding of the business direction. Despite all the changes, the survey indications continued to be positive. The culture transformation continues to unfold as the needs of the business dictate.

It is too soon to say that transformation has occurred, but the signs are evident. There is an entrepreneurial spirit in GTE that is growing, as is the business. There is greater hope and confidence in the company's ability to win in the marketplace than ever before. The press and Wall Street are also concurring in greater numbers. Much of the change is being led from the top, but more than ever before, it is coming from the grassroots.

# VI.

# Implications for the Future

In the first decades of the twenty-first century, we will learn the extent to which the end of the twentieth century created the groundwork for new patterns of work. This new groundwork would include laying the foundations for organizational learning in an environment requiring rapid adaptation to new technology and radically changing market forces, both domestically and internationally.

Similarly, this period will be recognized for recasting the received wisdom governing team dynamics. Teams in the twenty-first century will know how to achieve high performance quickly–forming, dissolving and reforming teams–as market conditions require. They will routinely work at great distances from one another, linked by powerful networks, rather than by proximity.

Accordingly, the new protocols for teams will not include the necessity for bonding over time nor for working side by side. These new teams will be bonded by commitment to goals, not by long-standing personal relationships. They will have portable skills, enabling rapid team effectiveness.

These team attributes and individual characteristics, while not yet prevalent today, are seen in high-tech industries where such a work ethic has been documented. Project teams coalesce around goals, acquire a great sense of ownership, and may put in 80 hours per week to get the job done. What they get back is pride of ownership. They see the fruits of their creativity in the products marketed and sold. More tangibly, they may receive highly lucrative incentives, in the form of bonuses and stock options. They take risks, put in great effort and perform from a sense of personal accountability and responsibility. At the end of the day, they more than likely believe the rewards were worth their efforts. Rapid proliferation of these teams won't happen over night. Much of what will enable such adaptability is being learned today.

It is no wonder then that there has been so much interest in learning organizations. Only those organizations that have already laid the groundwork for change are beginning to reap the benefits. Achieving rapid change is possible only when the organizational pump has been primed and the infrastructure of vision, leadership, empowerment and people-supporting practices has been realized.

Without a holistic approach, organizational change cannot take hold. Whether restructuring, downsizing or reengineering, all organizational systems require consideration. While one can reengineer processes relatively quickly, people take longer. Reengineering business processes may be revolutionary, but changing corporate culture is typically evolutionary.

There is no body of literature today that provides a "how to" for rapid culture change; however, there are emerging trends in organizations. When these trends are brought together, they begin to tell the story of how learning organizations are rewriting what we know about achieving high performance quickly in response to shifting market conditions.

An essential factor lies in structure. Horizontal structures create the needed flexibility. Organized by process rather than by function, horizontal structures foster greater coordination and integration and therefore faster response to competitive demands. Another critical factor for speed to market is the existence of powerful systems that can share data quickly up, down and across the organization. But equally important is the belief that the front line must have access to information and the power to make decisions based on that data in the service of the customer.

The organizations of tomorrow, facing competition from around the world, cannot afford labor strife in their home markets. We are likely to see a renewed vigor in the battle between labor and management. At the heart of this battle is a fundamental truth that goes beyond downsizing, mergers and restructuring. The heart of the battle is the past fighting against the implications of the future. The future is dictating an environment in which age-old relationships based on self-interest and antagonism will be put aside for the larger issue of survival against increasing globalization and competition. This new relationship will require balancing self-interest with the larger interest of the survival of the enterprise.

At the same time, jobs are changing drastically. Old skills will not meet the demands of the future. Innovative corporate leaders recognize that continuous commitment to education and training is not a cost but an investment. Employees are recognizing that they cannot rely on the "boss" to provide all the answers regarding their own futures. Forward-thinking employees are taking their futures into their own hands and are plotting their course by ensuring current skills and contribution to the bottom line. Forward-thinking leaders are encouraging and supporting such efforts by making sure their employees have access to the required tools.

## The Future Possibility

The myriad personal identification numbers, phone numbers and access codes of our present-day lives are all part of systems and networks that don't talk to one another. The organizations of the future will be linked by integrated voice, video and data networks running more fluidly than we can even imagine today.

The implications of this technology on the work force of tomorrow are staggering. There is every potential for the future of work to be truly democratic–all voices capable of being heard–unleashing new levels of involvement with greater creativity and innovation than ever before.

There may be a truth prevalent at that time that appears as a paradox to us today: the sense of community that may emerge from the virtual organizations of the future. The seeds of that future are in the soil of today's organizations. The emerging leaders are tending their gardens today.

# References

1. Cooperrider, David L. and Suresh Srivastava, eds. *Appreciative Management and Leadership*. San Francisco, California: Jossey-Bass, 1990, p. 35.

2. Barrett, Frank. "Creating Appreciative Learning Cultures." *Organization Dynamics,* 1995, Vol. 24, p. 36.

3. Senge Peter. *The Fifth Discipline: The Art & Practice of the Learning Organization,* New York, New York: Doubleday/Currency, 1990, p. 45.

4. Garvin, David A. "Building a Learning Organization." Harvard Business Review, July–August 1993, p. 45.

# Further Reading


Argyris, C. and D. A. Schon, eds. *Organizational Learning.* Reading, Massachusetts: Addison-Wesley, 1978.

Barrett, Frank. "Creating Appreciative Learning Cultures." *Organization Dynamics.* 1995, Vol. 24, pp 36–49.

Cooperrider, David L. "The 'Child' as Agent of Inquiry." *OD Practitioner.* 1996, Vol. 28 (1/2), pp 5–10.

Cooperrider, David L. "Resources for Getting Appreciative Inquiry Started: An Example OD Proposal." *OD Practitioner.* 1996, Vol. 28 (1/2), pp 23–32.

Cooperrider, David L. and Suresh Srivastava. "Appreciative Inquiry in Organizational Life." *Research in Organizational Change and Development.* 1987, Vol 1, pp. 129–169.

Cooperrider, David L. and Suresh Srivastava, eds., "Positive Image, Positive Action: The Affirmative Basis of Organizing." *Appreciative Management and Leadership,* San Francisco, California: Jossey Bass, 1990.

Cooperrider, David L and Diana Whitney, eds., *Workbook of Appreciative Inquiry,* Case Western University, Department of Organization Behavoir, 1996.

Garvin, David A., "Building a Learning Organization." *Harvard Business Review,* July–August, 1993.

Hamel, Gary and C. K. Prahalad, *Competing for the Future,* Boston, Massachusetts: Harvard Business School Press, 1994.

Pascale, Richard Tanner and Anthony G. Athos, *The Art of Japanese Management: Applications for American Executives,* New York, New York: Simon & Schuster, 1981.

Senge, Peter M., *The Fifth Discipline: The Art and Practice of the Learning Organization.* New York, New York: Doubleday/Currency, 1990.

Senge, Peter M., Charlotte Roberts, Richard B. Ross, Bryan J. Smith, and Art Kleiner, *The Fifth Discipline Fieldbook.* New York, New York: Doubleday, 1994.

# About the Authors

Nancy J. Burzon has multiple responsibilities in her current position as Director, Leadership Development and Employee Learning for GTE Corporation. In her position, she provides the corporate-wide education support for strategic objectives of organizational transformation and culture change, leadership and management development, quality performance and internal expansion.

In the course of her career with GTE, she has acquired experience in national account sales, sales management, market planning, business development, and strategic planning.

Nancy graduated from the University of Tennessee with a Bachelor of Arts in Psychology.

Nancy is a member of the Board of Directors and serves as Treasurer of the International Service Quality Association (ISQA), an organization which brings together executives from companies recognized for their superior quality of service to customers and academicians recognized for their cutting edge work in the service quality discipline for the purpose of continuous learning and improvement. She is a contributing author to *The Service Quality Handbook,* published in 1994, and *Teamworking and Quality Improvement; Lessons from British and North American Organizations* published in 1997.

Nancy J. Burzon, GTE Corporation
1255 Corporate Drive, Irving, TX 75038

Jean Moore is the assistant vice president for design and advanced learning systems for GTE. In her current role, she is responsible for integrating all curriculum design, advanced systems development, and external learning alliances and partnerships. In her previous position at GTE, she was the practice leader for workforce effectiveness, where she led change and culture initiatives.

Jean joined GTE in 1984 as a management development instructor. Since that time, she has held positions in the areas of organization and management development, organization effectiveness and employee relations for GTE Corporation, GTE Data Services and GTE Telephone Operations. Prior to joining GTE, Jean was a college professor, having earned her Ph.D. in 1981. She has made presentations on change management to companies benchmarking GTE and to audiences at numerous professional conferences. Some of these include: AQP, San Antonio, Texas, 1995; QUIS 5 (Quality in Services Symposium), Karlstad, Sweden, 1996; Phoenix (Michael Hammer Working Session), Dallas, Texas, 1996; Business Process Re-engineering/People Practices, to meet benchmarking requests from: Quebec Telephone, August 1994; PacBell, November 1994; Deutsche Telekom, April 1995. She was an invited speaker, along with David Cooperrider, at the October 1997 ODN (Organizational Development Network) conference in Scottsdale, Arizona. In addition, Jean is co-owner of GTE's Culture Inititiative, which won an Excellence In Practice Award at the 1998 ASTD conference in San Francisco.

Jean P. Moore, GTE Corporation
One Telecom Parkway, Temple Terrace, FL 33637